D1798502

Safety First!

by Meish Goldish

SCHOOL PUBLISHERS

Printed in China

ISBN 10: 0-15-350314-9
ISBN 13: 978-0-15-350314-6

Ordering Options
ISBN 10: 0-15-349941-9 (Grade 6 ELL Collection)
ISBN 13: 978-0-15-349941-8 (Grade 6 ELL Collection)
ISBN 10: 0-15-357358-9 (package of 5)
ISBN 13: 978-0-15-357358-3 (package of 5)

5 6 7 8 9 10   0940   12 11 10 09

Every summer, thousands of people go to the wilderness for a good hike along a forest trail. America has fifty-six national parks and hundreds more state parks. These parks contain just about every type of land found in the northern hemisphere.

Some of the most popular day hikes are through wooded areas. What could be more peaceful than to rest against a thick tree trunk as the sun comes through the leaves. The day is hot. You reach for your water bottle, and . . . Yikes!

A big spider is sitting on the bottle! The spider looks perfectly happy. However, you are not sure you want to share your water with a spider. There are only a few species of poisonous spiders in America. This spider is probably perfectly harmless. However, check with an adult on your hike to make sure. Then you can give the water bottle a gentle shake. The spider will probably scurry off.

The red hourglass shape on this spider tells you it is a poisonous black widow.

Tick

There are other kinds of potentially harmful insects to watch for in the wilderness. Ticks are insects you should be careful to avoid. Ticks are found in tall grasses and in the woods. Ticks can attach themselves to humans and animals. One kind of tick can give people a disease called Lyme Disease. Lyme Disease can be treated with medication. However, it's better to avoid ticks altogether. It is recommended that hikers wear light-colored clothing to better see dark-colored ticks. Also, ticks won't be able to bite skin they can't get to. Wear long pants tucked into your socks and shirts with long sleeves. Check yourself for ticks when you return home from a hike. Have an adult help you remove any tick you find.

Most hikers carry a food pack with them. Even a can of cold beans or a squashed sandwich tastes great in the wilderness. Be sure to pack your lunch in a waterproof container in case your backpack falls in some water. You can use the container to carry out all of your garbage. High-energy foods like granola are good to have on all hikes!

A word about water before you start on your hike. Actually, two words about water: *Be smart*. It is always best to carry your own water. That way you know the water is safe to drink. You might be able to see to the bottom of a clear mountain lake. However, that does not mean the water is safe to drink. The same is true for those crystal clear streams. Most of America's lakes and rivers contain high amounts of bacteria. Bacteria can make you very sick.

If you do not want to carry water then it is important to carry a good water filter. A water filter takes the larger germs and debris out of the water so that you can drink it safely. Iodine kills most germs that are too small to be filtered out. Just remember this: drink only water that you bring with you or water that is purified with a water filter and iodine.

Okay, it is time to get going on our hike. Is everybody ready? Let's check our list of things to take along on our hike.

 **Protective clothing**

Sunscreen

 **Food in waterproof containers**

Pure water or a filter and iodine tablets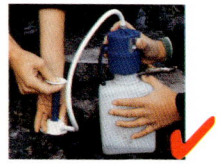

 **Insect repellent**

Map — we'll get to that later, but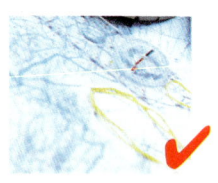

It looks like we are ready to go . . .

Oops! There is your family dog, staring at you. Perhaps it has its leash in its mouth. The dog knows something big is happening. The dog certainly does not want to be left out! What should you do?

Only you and your family know your dog's behavior. Is the dog old and slow and better off at home taking a nap on its favorite rug? Is the dog a young puppy with the desire but not yet the manners to go on a hike? Sometimes it is kinder to leave the pet at home.

However, if your dog can handle a full day along a forest path, you might be able to take the dog along. National parks and many state parks do not allow dogs, so you will have to check with the park to find out whether dogs are allowed on the walk you have chosen. If they are allowed, be sure to bring extra water for your dog. Always keep your dog on a leash. Your dog may want to protect you from a bear, or a skunk, or even a cow if you are in cattle country. An encounter with an animal could be very dangerous for both you and your dog. When in doubt, leave furry friends at home.

If you should come upon a bear, there are some important things to remember. First, all bears should always be considered dangerous, especially if a bear is with its cubs. A mother bear will always try to protect her cubs. If you are in bear country, wear bells or carry two sticks to hit together to make noise. Make lots of noise especially if you are coming around a corner. The bear will hear you coming. It will most likely run off. Never run if you meet up with a bear. Stand very still until hopefully the bear gets bored and walks away.

Skunks are another possible problem in the woods. Startled skunks can create an odor that is strong enough to sting your (and your dog's) eyes. At the least, you will go home smelling very bad! There are special products for removing the smell from both you and your dog. Hold your dog's leash tight if you see a skunk. Remain still until the skunk walks away.

Perhaps this last bit of advice should have been on the first page! Do you know where you are going on your hike? Maps are extremely helpful in getting where you want to go. Also, maps help you find your way home again. Most parks have maps you can take with different routes marked on them. The maps will tell you what kind of terrain you will be walking through and how long the hike will be. The maps also often describe some of the plants and animals you might see along the way.

I think it is time to start. There is just one more thing to check: √ have fun!

Scaffolded Language Development

INTERROGATIVE SENTENCES Tell students that an interrogative sentence asks a question. Remind students that in English, a question mark is used at the end of a sentence that is a question. Review the following interrogative sentences from the selection, modeling using the correct intonation:

What should you do? (page 9)

Is the dog old and slow and better off at home taking a nap on its favorite rug? (page 10)

Have students chorally read the interrogative sentences aloud using intonation appropriate for asking a question. Have students find interrogative sentences in the selection and take turns reading them aloud fluently using the appropriate intonation. Ask students to write five interrogative sentences using a question mark. Have students read each other's sentences aloud.

Science

Poisonous Spiders The black widow was mentioned in the text as an example of a poisonous spider that is found in the United States. Have students research another poisonous spider that is found in the United States. Have them draw a picture of the spider and list facts about the spider, such as where it can be found and how to identify it.

School-Home Connection

Safety Procedures Have students discuss with a family member what safety procedures they should practice at home. How can they help younger members of their family practice safety?

Word Count: 1,073